Tree of Metamorphoses

Tree of Metamorphoses

AUDREY McHUGH

RESOURCE *Publications* • Eugene, Oregon

TREE OF METAMORPHOSES

Copyright © 2022 Audrey McHugh. All rights reserved. Except for brief quotations in critical publications or reviews, no part of this book may be reproduced in any manner without prior written permission from the publisher. Write: Permissions, Wipf and Stock Publishers, 199 W. 8th Ave., Suite 3, Eugene, OR 97401.

Resource Publications
An Imprint of Wipf and Stock Publishers
199 W. 8th Ave., Suite 3
Eugene, OR 97401

www.wipfandstock.com

PAPERBACK ISBN: 978-1-6667-5361-5
HARDCOVER ISBN: 978-1-6667-5362-2
EBOOK ISBN: 978-1-6667-5363-9

11/03/22

Grateful acknowledgment is made to the editors of the journals and anthologies who first published the following poems. The poems, sometimes in earlier versions, appeared as follows:

The National Society of American Pen Woman Magazine: "Spring in the Pandemic"; *Sierra Club Poetry*, newsletter and on-line: "Heedless," "Laudato Si," "The Redwood Grove," b.j. Spoke Gallery: "The Redwood Grove," "The Toll."

Barnes Gallery; "Tree of Metamorphoses, "Truth or Dare", "War Without End".

Special thanks to my intrepid editor, April Ossman, who fit my book into her honeymoon.

To the ones who loved me first, Olive & Austin
To the ones who loved me best, Charlie & Gert
To the ones who loved me most, Beth, Joe, Tom, Katie
Tony, Marie, Nancy, Diane

"And as the imagination bodies forth
The forms of things unknown, the poet's pen
Turns them to shapes and gives to airy nothing
A local habitation and a name."

A Midsummer Night's Dream
William Shakespeare

Contents

I

Worlds Unknown	3
Truth or Dare	4
Chance	5
Taken	6
Betrayal	7
Come from Away	8
We Gather Together	9
The Toll	10
Prodigal Son	11
A Moment in Time	12
Good News/ Bad News	13
Tahlequah's Wake	14
Family Lore	15
Spring in the Pandemic	16
Climbing Mt. Sinai	17
The New Normal	18
My Birthday Wish	19
Heedless	20
Final Hopes	21
A Hopeful Toast	22

II

Violets	25
The Space Age	26

CONTENTS

Darfur 2003	27
Black Lives Matter	28
Pandemic	29
Searching for God in Far Away Places	30
War Without End	31
The Redwood Grove	32
Famine	33
Tiger as Captive	34
Setting Sail	35
Out, out, Brief Candle	36
Huddled Masses	37
Contagion	38

III

Heard	41
One Day	42
Young Death	43
Dawn Alive	44
A Toast to Love's Labor	45
The Mallards	47
Babylon, by Argyle Lake	48
Time Passing	49
Laudato Si	50
Alone	51
Daybreak	52
Good Morning	53
A Toast for Katie	54
Spirit	55
Widowhood	56
Evolution	57
The Family Tree	59
Metamorphoses	60
Notes	61

I

Worlds Unknown

The Milky Way's horizon event
seen searching for a dual universe,
beyond chemistry to biology,
suggests to some
a theological cosmos,
just as NASA searches the void
with its Kepler telescope
spying for earth-like worlds,
amid planets of ice and fire,
thirsting for water-worlds,
obscured by strange black holes,
looking for life in the goldilocks zone,
wondering if we're alone.

Truth or Dare

With Virgil at my side, I verge
on humankind's dizzying depths,
to face a truth that dares not hide
behind the mask of certainty,
and see a world not meant to be
slouching toward eternity,
cityscapes of begging hands
in search of good Samaritans.
On dirty streets we pass the homeless by,
side-stepping needle pricks
of conscience in seeing these men
left behind, their dreams long gone,
and those that still abide
haunting every hungry eye.

Chance

The realm of the golden eagle
pierces a granite-rimmed sky,
where wind is colder, sharper
than the Matterhorn peaks.

He eyes some young marmots
stilled, a chasm's depth below
riveted, his purpose set
on the rocks where they died:

But roaring down upon them,
the avalanche at noon,
did suffocate the funeral feast,
and blanket every bloom.

Taken

For many years I whispered *Billy*,
half prayer, half lament,

over the cradle in my attic,
his silky lock of hair.

Who is to blame for arms
that bear the loss,

empty as an amputation,
where phantom pain remains:

"After the first death
There is no other," says it best

through the years I asked why
a child should die,
but no answer came—
or maybe I was deaf to it.

Betrayal

Past days of presumed honesty, decayed
like composting flowers in the rain,
when children were understood to be
beyond the wick of passion's flame.
Now we see in defilement of priest's chastity,
a crime so hellish against the innocent,
as to burn unfurled petals from ever blooming,
cloistering their lives in haunting bitter years,
while sham saints withering smiles
above high collars can't deny
their loathsome deeds exhumed.

Come from Away

Roaming the hills of Newfoundland,
I hear the lilt of my mother's voice,
telling the stories she told to me
along the road to Salmonier,
of Uncle Mike and his sons,
drowning on the Bonnie Lass,
and his wife who searched the sea,
and the many years she prayed.

I hear at the water's edge,
secrets echoed in the waves
and gray skies above mourning
their spirits, entangled in sunken tombs
telling the shore in some foreign tongue
what they never shared with us.

We Gather Together

Sliding on Churchill's slippery ice,
blinded by minus-thirty biting snow
blowing through the parking field,
we navigated our way to the observatory,
where we waited to transcend
mundane aches and pains.
Soon a celestial display appeared,
mesmerizing us with undulating red,
green, blue and yellow light,
described as electrical particles
charged by the sun's energy,
but known to the native Cree nation
as their ancestors, the Salamiut,
performing their sun dance in the sky,
happy to see them again,
the solar wind conducting them
in a heavenly rendition
of We Gather Together,
sung in their forbidden native tongue,
but known to us as the Aurora Borealis.
We chased with our gazes
the changing hues, darting
translucent beauty, playing
a celestial game of family tag.
Too soon, the ghostly ancestors
faded back into the past, to await
the imagination of new generations.

The Toll

Haunted melodies echo the woodlands
on a breeze of stunted pines,
the boring of weevils and aphids
are the sounds of warning signs.

The meadows and wheatfields will mourn
in the heat of summer's increasing oppression,
the loss of monarch butterflies
and the flowers and plants they pollinate.

We long to walk green lands again,
to remove the gray shrouding our cities,
letting skyscrapers see the sunlight
through the clouds, reaching for heaven.

To save us from mass extinctions,
the lost call out our names
to change the fate they hear tolling,
before the path of our passing is paved.

Prodigal Son

Walking with you through
the arboretum's nurtured blooms,
I hoped the sheltered sky would pardon
 years lost in bickering and blame,
that hardened the stones of a son's resentment.
 As I reached for your hand in renewed trust,
we grasped beyond time, the pain of my need
 for a father's love, too lately given.

Soon after, we met again,
with another pain between us,
your newly enfeebled hand,
sliding too soon from mine—
I know violets will return to bloom
fathers and sons will go astray,
but does memory last up heavens way?

A Moment in Time

We startled each other,
as he emerged from primordial forest:
my fearful eyes meeting his curious gold,
only twenty feet away, as I bent,
exhausted by my climb.
A gray wolf, an apex predator intent
on his mysterious mission,
circling us in a purposeful gait.
We watched in awe as he loped past,
back through Yellowstone's
radiant lupines, back to majestic forest,
stunning us into silence,
while something untamed in us
settled into gratitude.

Good News/ Bad News

Political pundits broadcasting the news
for simple souls to choose —
his truth, my truth, or science.
If one photo of a weeping glacier
is worth a thousand words
how many truths is that?
More protests today, or is it fake news,
but life goes on, or does it—
under floods, heat waves, and blazing forests?
the weather channel with no sunny days,
Greta Thunberg, meet Joan of Arc,
igniting the spark for the children's crusade.
Let Pope Francis march with Cardinal Burke,
amid hymns and banners for peace on Earth
as the temperature rises, the challenging times
of synodals in peace will be sanctified.

Tahlequah's Wake

The sickly whale, newly birthed,
ascending on her still soft fins,
breaks through the polluted waters
to gasp the sullen air of Earth,
as her malnourished mother, sister, all her kin,
unaware of nature's manmade dearth,
whistle in their native tongue
the song of afterbirth.

As the little calf slipped beneath the waves,
Tahlequah raised upon her head
the life she tried but couldn't save.
After weeks of swimming as a bier,
she released her burden,
and the calf descended to the depths
we plumbed so wantonly.

Family Lore

From failing crops and misery,
to endurance in adversity,
they sailed, remembering their Irish wakes,
forsaking green fields and streams,
boarding the fearsome ship
leaving Liverpool.
They shared their meager rations,
with hands long grown pale
from hunger in their famished land,
and thirst for a forbidden language.
Britannic broke the ocean's waves,
for these unbroken Gaels,
as told in their tales of crossing
the Atlantic's wind-driven sea.
Segregated in decks below,
these huddled masses prevailed,
"For each age is a dream that is dying
Or one that is coming to birth."

Spring in the Pandemic

The primrose path blooms again
and lilies of the fields raise
their blooms like praying hands.
The shamrock grows for the Trinity,
when our fears yield to faith,
Spring sprouting from Aaron's staff
still finds the sun;
the rose of Sharon in Eden's garden
resurrected for a breathless world,
to those who wait in hope.

Climbing Mt. Sinai

We venture climbing at midnight,
full moon our only illumination
in this desolate place.
Following shadows in the dust,
I hike in haste, to keep my friends
in sight, stumbling till my eyes adjust,
rocks slipping beneath my feet
like a trial of belief,
as the dark shades to gray
and wind dries the fine rime of sweat on my uplifted face.
We rest in a makeshift tent,
hearing different languages
spoken by people with a single purpose,
then push on for two more hours,
arriving at the summit to see the sun rise,
the same sun that shone on Moses,
the same wind that blew on his face,
walking the same earth in his footsteps,
praying to the same loving God.

The New Normal

The living have abandoned
both broad and narrow streets,
ghosted by a few distant, cringing
grocery shoppers hoping not to touch.
Fear is the very marrow
that death may set us free,
as the ambulance I heard today,
might be coming back for me.

Yesterday a homeless man
approached me cautiously—
he knows the people praying here
may call the police on seeing
his fowl clothes and dirty hands,
a truth that yet may prove to be:
homelessness and hunger
may be coming back for me.

My Birthday Wish

I want to feel time in my hands,
not sand as in the hourglass,
not leaking through my fingers,
but cupped in generous palms.

I want my birthday bell to ring
so loud it dims this age of infernos,
and apocalyptic floods,
upstaging the stage of politics.

I want to have my own parade,
beyond the sound of big brass bands,
to live a life whose total span
bridges the gift of love.

Heedless

From the morning just born from night sky,
comes a torrent of acid rain,
falling by the wayside on the road to ruin.
We see vanishing species and stygian seas,
searching for blue whale fins and harlequin frogs,
in Sylvan oceans and clear, clean streams .
Hope was not enough for the spotted owl
and passenger pigeon.
The oil of earth and dirt of coal,
the city's invasion of wildlife's home,
creating a concrete gas land,
ensuring for some species a day of extinction.
Conscience yet may prove to be
the bellwether for biodiversity.
After the ambush of former days is gone,
what lies ahead, what beyond?

Final Hopes

To thrust my hand in a cold running stream,
reflecting the forest's green canopy.
To write a poem like Whitman's
Lilacs Last in the Dooryard Bloom'd.
To swim with the dolphins, fly with the birds,
and kiss a wild animal home.
To float in a hot air balloon over Nefertiti's tomb.
To crack my hermitically sealed opinions
with the incision of an open mind.
To love my family, my country, my God,
a pledge that surely will retell
Washington's deathbed affirmation, "*Tis Well.*"

A Hopeful Toast

To all the civilians who ever marched,
their voices heard in words of protest,
against prejudice and injustice.

These deserving citizens of our promised land ,
inspired by Buffalo Soldiers in their talkative tombs,
whispering that the stony road of suffering
will one day become the path that "We shall overcome."

Martin Luther King's dream will be fulfilled,
when another Marion Anderson sings
for the Daughters of the American Revolution.

When civil rights are had by all,
Juneteenth and brotherhood embraced,
the final battle of the Civil War will be won.

II

Violets

Stumbling in the stubby grass,
I grab a stranger's headstone
to steady my feet,
before finding my father's grave,
moldering in summer heat.

Twenty years today have passed
since the wounds I caused,
the folly of words remembered
deepens my sorrow as we meet,
too late to ask forgiveness.

Can you smell your favorite flower?
Violets bloom this very hour,
near the stone bridge, still fragrant,
where I trod them on my way,
clinging fast to the heel that crushed them.

The Space Age

One day a great diaspora to be,
evolved in future time and tense,
will dream of leaving life on Earth,
past mapped stars with a fuller sense
of destiny, and know the worth
of humankind, when taken hence,
reseeding the dust of our rebirth,
and earthrise seen as recompense.

Darfur 2003

A mother's life of suffering
has met a violent end.
Her broken body bleeding
upon the shaming ground,
along with dead men
still bound hand and foot,
fallen where survivors heard
her baby's cries, still feeding
at her dying breast.
The survivors plot their revenge,
honor bound in their darkness,
until soon another village,
quiet in another dawn,
awaits another bloody fate,
and another mother's life is taken.

Black Lives Matter

On shared streets we shout his name,
dying needlessly upon the ground,
his soft neck choked
by the knee of white authority,
pleading, Stop, I can't breathe,
ignored and unrelieved,
a dream seemingly became
yet another hangman's tale,
a woven rope of hate and fear,
without the tree, but the throat was there.

On shared streets we say, *George Floyd*,
our sense of shame too long delayed.
Father, son, and friend destroyed,
"I have a dream to one day be,"
silenced in its infancy,

A global voice came to raise him,
like a phoenix from the dead,
if only he could hear
the multitude calling his name.

Pandemic

We see more than a trace
of cruel truth in our human face,
of emotions masked behind contagion's veil.
Devoid of touch, our spirits
wilt like flowers in drought,
thirsting for embrace.
Echoing through the quiet world,
the trumpet of unremitting loss.
Millions rest in the loneliest of sleeps,
followed by burials none may attend.
We post instead on social media,
our virtual lilies of loving memory,
while grief stands alone at the grave.

Searching for God in Far Away Places

I hear a place beyond the stars
where angels call my name,
if only I could see it clearly,
as the Kepler telescope
views Jupiter and Mars,
or feel the solar wind
embrace my esoteric mind,
leaving all my doubts
imbedded in a cosmic milieu,
as Andromeda unbound
in her celestial constellation,
looking for any human trace
in stardust left behind,
finding my way in outer space
redeemed, unknowing why,
blinded by shooting stars,
immersed in inter-stellar grace.

War Without End

Mourning Ukraine's new devastation
engenders memories of how Chamberlain's
promise of peace became a paper chase,
espoused over soldiers bleeding
in open fields, his politics crushed
like Poland under power's heel.
Appeasement paved the path
for marching feet at war,
when nations' brave and ablest men
lay dead on alien shores.
Millions of souls mowed
like so much grass,
as Germany fed her ovens,
with no such qualms as Macbeth,
no matter how many haunt him.
A just call to arms, but still plagued
by human waste and mourning,
the Trojan horse of war and peace
hiding an endless fight for freedom.

The Redwood Grove

Once a timeless redwood grove,
whose green leaves waved in the sunlight,
red sturdy trunks that outlived
the birth and death of nations,
their gnarled feet wicks
that fire blackened, but did not consume,
these survivors of glacial freeze
and devastating drought,
have met a violent end.

Felled by wanton lumbering,
on a scale measured in human greed,
Earth's tallest trees crashed on the ground,
their dismembered branches left to rot,
abandoned by the hummingbird and bees,
mourned by the goldfinch, warbler,
and mountains that know they're gone.

Redwood dust clings to hikers
walking in the graveyard,
amid the ruins of the tree's cathedral,
its sanctuary littered
with barren stumps and stones,
once an avian paradise
where humans came to worship.

Famine

The wasteland dries them to the bone,
as locusts further strip famine fields,
pleasing death, who drags whole families home.

Children ask why wheat won't grow,
why clouds withhold their rain,
as the wasteland dries them to the bone.

Hungry voices chorus primal moans,
begging among those well-fed,
pleasing death, who drags them home.

Until foreign cameras make them known,
they live in fading hope,
as the wasteland dries them to the bone.

The children's vacant eyes are shown
to a world beyond their seeing,
pleasing death, who drags them home.

A hunger unknown in rich nations,
though change may come in climate storms,
as new wastelands dry them to the bone,
pleasing death, who drags them home.

Tiger as Captive

No longer burning bright,
scarce in *"forests of the night,"*
your cage obscures the sky,
and dims the fire of your eyes.

The burning furnace of your brain,
banked, encumbered by your chains.
Apex predator of nature's bounty,
tamed from *"fearful symmetry."*

The *"immortal hand"* that made your fire
reflected wonder, God's desire,
alas for human innocence lost
in nailing nature to our cross.

Setting Sail

At Southards Pond,
we stopped near the bridge,
though it was getting late,
to sail our sticks, broken and bent,
downstream, where Katie asked,
Nana, where is the sunset sent?
and, *Why do fish need bait?*

Knowing what she really meant,
and nature needing no debate,
we went home to eat our supper,
wondering where the stream
sent our missives.

Remembering that day years later,
I wonder what unconscious need
prompted us to launch
such signs of brokenness and loss,
realized soon enough in her mother's
suffering and sudden death,
when the journey to each sunset
seemed endless.

Out, out, Brief Candle

Scarcely moving her sunken eyes,
and tabby golden head,
which nightly lifted my willing hand,
her purring lullabied us to sleep.
Once, she scampered around the house,
rescued from life lived by sun and moon,
wild by nature before we met as friends,
gentle Shakespeare, once a poet
of feline motion, you will not die alone,
and if we ever meet again,
as Pharaohs believed of cats and men,
bring an amphora for my tears.

Huddled Masses

They climbed aboard one clear midnight,
quietly, so no one could hear,
and arrest their progress.
They came with names and faces,
the banished children of that ancient land.
The Kurdi family must have huddled together
fearfully, trembling on the overloaded rubber boat,
which sank within minutes of its launch.
Three-year-old Alan was found
face-down on sand lapped by waves,
tiny sneakers still on both feet,
blue shorts like the ones I bought my son.
They came with names and faces,
today's "huddled masses
yearning to breathe free,"
none deserved betrayal.

Contagion

This blunt force trauma
is bearing down upon us,
finding in every circle
of family and friends a nail.
The viral hammer
keeps striking suddenly,
landing without a care
on the lonely and beloved,
shocking unbelieving hearts,
too late to mend, too late for prayer,
too much to bear.

III

Heard

I hear passerine melodies
both present and past,
where every tree is home to me,
sheltering my dreams and sorrows.
Once I carved my name in this maple tree,
giving me a model to embrace equally
the day and night,
lifting leafy arms in prayer.
Long past the days of my ego's rule,
with its wild and winning ways,
I greet my longing, grown green at last,
spent of ambition's unwise desires,
having made peace with existential mysteries.
Encouraged by your faithful words
in a missive mailed a world apart,
landing in my greenest valley
of answered prayers.

One Day

Amid wild grass at twilight,
a vision in stillness reflected whole,
but scattered in ripples,
shimmering plumage wet,
a solitary egret, white in the willows,
surprises my peripheral vision—
seeing me as I do her,
moving in shadows,
startling each other-
she takes off, wings splashing,
soaring aloft above the lake,
in perfect form, lithe in flight
as I hope one day to be.

Young Death

Despite the promises of poets,
I will never be the same:
left abandoned by sudden death,
some grief eludes all taming.
It may be chained to sturdy posts,
but ready to break free
when I need your memory most,
or sleeping to give respite
from daily life,
reasons to go on breathing,
for other friends and needs,
and my need to hear
your name spoken again,
my need to keep our memories unbroken.

Dawn Alive

Returning red-winged blackbirds
forage among last year's weeds,
robins hop on the lawn
in search of early worms,
cardinals sing from the tallest tree,
an avian conclave in morning prayer.
Awakened from slumber,
the warming earth breaks winter's silence
with creaking limbs
and trickling snowmelt,
as new life emerges into the dangerous air,
alive with every possibility
in heard and unheard melodies.

A Toast to Love's Labor

To all the boys I've loved before,
to the one who loved me first,
and held me in his arms at night
to satisfy my thirst.

Sweets for the next one,
who held my hand
reluctantly at first,
then with a shy, awkward smile,
my brother loved me best.

Tears for boyfriends I practiced on,
then kissed and left behind,
and those whose egos
always wanted more,
and promised only lies.

Last, a toast beyond champagne,
to marriage with my life's partner.
We attended hockey games
and Sunday mass together,
when sometimes he'd rather
be catching up on sleep,
as he often did,
riding to work on the railroad.

His fatherly hands
built our skating rink,
for sons who never knew
the cost of his love's labor:
his last will and testament.

The Mallards

Their quacking racket
like a jazz band of muted saxes,
playing for nature's sake,
or maybe just the sunny day,
rouses my standing ovation
for their brassy display.

Daily at sundown they fly
in perfect winged formation,
to shelter in shallows
near the bay.

I watch them soar,
their glossy green
and chestnut bodies
reflected in the icy lake,
my wonderment obscured
by brimming eyes.

Babylon, by Argyle Lake

  My hometown is a lovely place:
the post office, the church,
morning walks along the lake,
old friendly faces,
though most only nod in silence,
lost in their own dreams
as I meditate, half awake,
on a life well-lived,
  the loves forsaken, the prayers unsaid,
my unsettled, sometimes turbulent life.
As I pass the waterfall,
its endless tumbling suggests
unplanned, unfinished,
may be wisdom's way.

Time Passing

Do I walk the heron's path
to find an ideal place for standing still,
or wade into the lake's embracing bath,
stalking its rippled fullness.
Do I fear my forthright wisdom
will grow silent with the years,
and brute truth's beauty
disfigured or re-aligned,
in the lost intensity
of my feeble mind,
aware of its own diminishment.
Will I keep in my flabby decline,
to youthful ideals of beauty—
or find in my layered lines
incarnate poetry.
Will I find when even these
fading Elysian fields are gone,
that life diminished soldiers on.

Laudato Si

Nature still speaks psalms
and proverbs yet unknown,
but Earth now has a sorrow,
that heaven may not heal.
Can acid rain be cleansed by prayer,
restored pure as when it came
from the mountain's stormy heights.
Pollution's earthly shroud
obscures the birth of extinction:

Soil's sacred spring betrayed,
as wheat's amber waves of glory groan,
and ocean foam reeks of oil and sewage.
The beloved beasts that won't be born
will deprive mankind of sustenance,
and the Eden we defiled,
an inheritance of fire and destruction.
As our world wears away,
we can only hope for a new genesis,
birthing a reclaimed home.

Alone

We know the bare bones of his life,
his quiet self-absorption,
a loving wife, a grief unspoken,
sealed his lips despite the cost.
But if we roll away the stone,
we may see the many years it took
for this mariner to die alone
so far from home.
Under heavy dust, we found a book
of crumbling pages, hidden memories
yellowed with age, and tucked inside,
a sepia photo of a stern beauty
and handsome groom,
their story only truly known
to him alone, as lost to us
as ocean foam each wave loses,
to the next subsuming it,
his grief's drifting mist
a veil through which
we couldn't glimpse him—
forgotten, abandoned,
he finally took his life,
to find his home.

Daybreak

Take off your shoes and socks
and run the shore with me
inhale lungfuls of fragrant ocean air,
let salt spray coat your hair,
and let the wind tangle it.
Hear turbulent waves crashing
in the living sand,
laugh at the seagull's boldness
in snatching tidbits from our lunch.

Dance to natures Ode to Joy

played by the wind and waves,
see in the morning's first shining:
"*What I do is me,*
My warmth is meant to share."

Good Morning

A new day's breakfast
served at sunrise to hungry birds,
hoping patience will be rewarded,
by finding worms wiggling in self-defense,
and fallen seeds hoping to grow.
A red-tailed hawk scans the unwary,
before descending from the heavens,
a few fish leap into the sunlight,
paying a mortal price for the view,
yet leaving enough of their kin
to school us on the beauty
of living to see another day.

A Toast for Katie

When my grown granddaughter
proclaims she wants to be a writer,
I can only offer a toast—
here's hoping your prose
and poetry transforms
the ordinary to the sublime.
Don't falter in your quest,
or accept other's limits;
slip past the sentries of reality,
into the realm of imagination and wonder,
as one who sees beyond the rose,
weaving a tapestry of language
that bewilders the sensible mind,
inspires the metaphysical,
and entertains the rest.

Spirit

I feel the raindrops on my face,
with their wet and windy taste,
the dew drying on my petals,
as pollinators buzz in the sun.
My beauty rises immortally,
from every new seed and spring.
Buffeted by wind and hail,
drought, and soft neglect.
I am the dappled green of leaves,
the honeypot of nature's sustenance.
I am the dream of years to fill
with faith to move your mountains.
I am the joy of tears gone by,
the fireside where love abides—
the suffering servant of biblical fame,
serving hope to humankind.
I am the spirit of life and death
forever abiding, though never spent.

Widowhood

I thought I heard his voice today,
though it was very dim,
sweet words of care and missing me,
in the tone I know so well.

I thought I felt his hand today,
resting gently on my own,
just a touch, then letting go,
enough to comfort mine.

I thought he blew his breath today,
drying tears on my cheeks,
a reminder of what I have lost,
and the love I have kept.

I thought I saw his face today,
reflected in the light,
whispering what he used to say:
I told you I was right.

Evolution

From the void, coming,
unknowing of its purpose.
From the depths, coming,
unmindful of molten rock's
expansion and contraction.
Seeding of the seas coming,
life growing in complexity.
Swimming and walking, coming,
adjusting to diversity.
Birthing, consciousness, coming,
body with soul infused.
Homo sapiens coming,
reasoning its mission,
good and evil coming,
spirit and ego emerging,
tested in adversity.
Past and future coming,
complicating the present.
Space and time coming,
conflating in the cosmos,
science and religion coming,
giving up the chain of secrets.
Axial age coming,
living in its loneliness,
death and dying coming
to all suddenly awakened,
Imago Dei coming,
revealing in its mission,

Gloria Dei coming,
evolution's final edition.

The Family Tree

The tree of life, exiled from Eden,
has become a half-way house for the sick and lame.
Overhead, its leaves and branches
are green with envy for the evergreens.
Drunks hang on its trunk for balance,
as the sober cast every pond for blame.
Forked tongues flap for war,
in the guise of peace,
while their armaments promise the same.
They say Eve failed the test, the apples decayed,
and gluttons finished the rest.
The narcissists gather for their nightly reflections,
in mirrors of beauty and shame.
Twisting underfoot, the vines and thorns
conspire to bring me to my knees.
Blowing through the breaking leaves,
a breathing spirit who believes
in the Master Gardener,
with shears to prune Medusa's snakes,
and make of me a human shape
beyond the grasp of family trees,
and Adam's pride.

Metamorphoses

When eternity draws my breath,
from life into some other dimension,
treat my death as parting
the fibers of my being,
a butterfly metamorphosis of biblical proportions.
Contemplate, like an anatomy student,
the hidden miracles of existence,
mid-wifing my spirit's next birth.
Will I awake in darkness and silent sorrow,
regretting the past, or wake in spirit realigned,
in a state of mystical being beyond infinite,
a cosmic spirit communing in an emerging universe,

"Awakened from the dream of life."

Notes

"Taken" quotes a line from Dylan Thomas, "A Refusal to Mourn the Death of a Child in London."

"Family Lore" quotes a line from Arthur O' Shaughnessy, "Ode."

"A Hopeful Toast" quotes a line from Charles Albert Tindley, "We Shall Overcome."

"Black Lives Matter" quotes a line from Martin Luther King, "I have a Dream."

"Tiger as Captive" quotes a line from William Blake, "Tiger, Tiger, Burning Bright."

"Daybreak" quotes a line from Gerard Manley Hopkins, "As Kingfishers Catch Fire Dragonflies Catch Flame."

"Metamorphoses" quotes a line from P.B. Shelley, "Adonis."

"Final Hopes" quotes a line from George Washington, "Tis Well."

"Huddled Masses" quotes a line from Emma Lazarus, "The New Colossus."